www.osha.gov

I0476486

Occupational Safety and Health Act of 1970

"To assure safe and healthful working conditions for working men and women; by authorizing enforcement of the standards developed under the Act; by assisting and encouraging the States in their efforts to assure safe and healthful working conditions; by providing for research, information, education, and training in the field of occupational safety and health..."

This publication provides a general overview of worker rights under the *Occupational Safety and Health Act* (OSH Act). This publication does not alter or determine compliance responsibilities which are set forth in OSHA standards and the OSH Act. Moreover, because interpretations and enforcement policy may change over time, for additional guidance on OSHA compliance requirements the reader should consult current administrative interpretations and decisions by the Occupational Safety and Health Review Commission and the courts.

This information will be made available to sensory-impaired individuals upon request. Voice phone: (202) 693-1999; teletypewriter (TTY) number: 1-877-889-5627.

Cover photo courtesy of the National Roofing Contractors Association.

Protecting Roofing Workers

U.S. Department of Labor
Occupational Safety and Health Administration

OSHA 3755-05 2015

U.S. Department of Labor

Disclaimer

This guidance document is not a standard
or regulation and it creates no new legal
obligations. The document is advisory in
nature, informational in content, and is
intended to assist employers in providing
a safe and healthful workplace. The
Occupational Safety and Health Act requires
employers to comply with safety and health
standards promulgated by OSHA or by a
state with an OSHA-approved state plan.
In addition, the Act's Section 5(a)(1), the
General Duty Clause, requires employers to
provide their workers with a workplace free
from recognized hazards likely to cause death
or serious physical harm. Employers can be
cited for violating the General Duty Clause if
there is a recognized hazard and they do not
take reasonable steps to prevent or abate the
hazard. However, failure to implement any
specific recommendations contained within
this document is not, in itself, a violation of
the General Duty Clause. Citations can only
be based on standards, regulations, and the
General Duty Clause.

Table of Contents

Purpose and Scope of this Guide

Falls are the leading cause of death in the construction industry, accounting for over 3,500 fatalities between 2003 and 2013. Falls from roofs accounted for nearly 1,200, or 34%, of the fall deaths during that period. Roofers encounter many hazards on the job, including hazards associated with working at heights and from ladders, power tools, electricity, noise, hazardous substances, and extreme temperatures. Unless these hazards are controlled by the employer, roofers risk serious injury, illness and death.

To protect workers on roofing jobs, employers must identify the hazards present and take steps to address them. This guide covers safe practices to prevent falls, other physical injuries, hazardous substance exposures, and injuries and illnesses related to environmental conditions.

Below is a table of frequently cited OSHA standards for roofing contractors during FY 2013.

OSHA Standards Frequently Cited During FY 2013 Inspections of Roofing Contractors (NAICS 238160)

Rank by Number of Citations Issued	Categories	Standard
1	Duty to have fall protection	1926.501
2	Ladder safety	1926.1053
3	Fall protection training requirements	1926.503
4	Eye and face protection	1926.102
5	General scaffold requirements	1926.451
6	General safety and health provisions	1926.20
7	Head protection	1926.100
8	Fall protection systems criteria and practices	1926.502

OSHA Standards Frequently Cited During FY 2013 Inspections of Roofing Contractors (NAICS 238160)

Rank by Number of Citations Issued	Categories	Standard
9	Ladder training requirements	1926.1060
10	Hazard Communication	1926.59 which refers to 1910.1200

Source: NAICS 238160 – Roofing Contractors, October 2012 through September 2013.

Plan, Provide, Train

Falls can be prevented and lives can be saved through three simple steps: "Plan, Provide and Train." See OSHA's Fall Prevention Campaign web page for resources to help prevent falls (www.osha.gov/stopfalls).

Here are some basic ideas for developing fall protection strategies for roofing operations.

- Employers need to "PLAN" ahead to get the job done safely — Employers need to develop a plan and ensure the proper equipment, material and appropriately trained workers are available.
  - Know the pitch of the roof and follow the appropriate standard.
    - Low slope roof – 4:12 slope or less – 29 CFR 1926.501(b)(10).
    - Steep roof – above 4:12 slope – 29 CFR 1926.501(b)(11).
- Employers must "PROVIDE" the right equipment — Employers must provide fall protection and the right equipment for the job, including the right kinds of ladders, scaffolds, and safety gear.
- Employers must "TRAIN" workers to use the equipment safely — Employers must train workers in hazard recognition and in

the care and safe use of ladders, scaffolds, fall protection systems, and other equipment they will be using on the job.

○ Understand the requirements of OSHA's Fall Protection standards at 29 CFR 1926, Subpart M, to protect workers exposed to falls six feet or more above a lower level.

○ Implement safe work practices to reduce the possibility of falls.

○ Supervise workers to ensure fall protection equipment is used and maintained correctly.

○ Lead by example. Employers, project managers, and supervisors should follow the rules they are responsible for enforcing.

Need help? Don't wait. Call your nearest local OSHA area Compliance Assistance Specialist (www.osha.gov/dcsp/compliance_assistance/cas.html) or Consultation Program office (www.osha.gov/consultation).

Getting Started with Roofing Safety

All employers in the construction industry must have a safety program. Contractors and employers who perform construction work must comply with standards in 29 CFR 1926, Subpart C, General Safety and Health Provisions, as well as other applicable

Photo courtesy of ACTA Safety & Peterson Dean Roofing

standards. The standards outline employers' responsibilities for initiating and maintaining a safety program that provides for frequent and regular inspections of job sites, materials, and equipment (29 CFR 1926.20(b)(2)) and for ensuring that workers are trained to recognize and avoid unsafe conditions (29 CFR 1926.21(b)(2)). Employers must provide training in a language and in a manner that workers can understand.

Fall Protection Requirements

Falls are the leading cause of work-related injuries and deaths among roofers. Working six feet or more above lower levels put roofers at risk for serious injury or death if they should fall. A lack of fall protection, damaged fall protection equipment, or improper setup will increase their risk of falling from height.

Fall Protection Training

Employers must provide fall protection training for all workers who may be exposed to fall hazards. The training must be conducted by a competent person and include information on how to recognize fall hazards and on what procedures to follow to minimize them (29 CFR 1926.503(a)). Training must address how to inspect, erect/disassemble, and maintain the fall protection equipment involved in the work (29 CFR 1926.503(a)(2)(ii)).

Retraining is required when previous training becomes obsolete due to changes in work conditions or fall protection systems or equipment. Retraining is also required when worker performance indicates a need for it (29 CFR 1926.503(c)).

Employers must certify that workers have been trained by documenting it in accord with 29 CFR 1926.503(b) – Certification of Training.

For additional information on what must be included in fall protection training, see 29 CFR 1926.503 – Training Requirements.

The Requirement to Provide Fall Protection

Using a Personal Fall Arrest System (PFAS)

Employers generally must provide fall protection if workers are exposed to a fall of 6 feet or more to a lower level. One form of fall protection is a personal fall arrest system (PFAS). When used properly, these systems will arrest a fall and prevent the worker from contacting a lower level. A PFAS consists of an anchor, a harness, and a lifeline or lanyard (usually with a deceleration device).

A PFAS must be used properly to be effective. Adjust the harness to fit snugly. The D-ring attachment for the harness should be centered between the worker's shoulder blades and the leg straps should be adjusted until they are snug.

Fall arrest systems must be designed and set up to prevent a worker from free falling more than 6 feet or contacting a lower level (e.g., the floor or the ground) (29 CFR 1926.502(d)(16)(iii)).

Body belts are not acceptable in a PFAS because they can cause serious injury during a fall (29 CFR 1926.502(d)).

The anchorage for a fall arrest system must be capable of supporting 5,000 pounds per worker attached or be designed, installed, and used under the supervision of a qualified person, as part of a complete personal fall arrest system that maintains a safety factor of at least two (29 CFR 1926.502(d)(15)). During roofing work, it is important not to attach anchors to sheathing, single trusses, or most guardrails. These are typically not strong enough to meet OSHA's standard. Instead of attaching anchors to sheathing alone, attach an anchor to a structural member by driving the fasteners through the sheathing and into the rafter or truss member below. It is important to follow the manufacturer's instructions when installing anchorage.

Employers must ensure that fall arrest equipment subjected to the forces of a fall are taken out of service until it has been inspected by a competent person and determined to be undamaged and suitable for reuse (29 CFR 1926.502(d)(19)).

How to Set Up a Personal Fall Arrest System

The length of the lifeline or lanyard, the position of the anchor, and the distance to the lower level are all important. Employers need to select equipment that permits workers to operate efficiently while limiting the distance they could fall.

Employers must properly calculate the fall clearance distance to ensure that a worker will not contact the lower level in the event of a fall (29 CFR 1926.502(d)(16)(iii)). And employers also need to evaluate the potential for a pendulum effect, which could swing a fallen worker into a nearby object. Swing-fall hazards can cause serious injuries, but they can be minimized by installing the anchorage point above the work area (i.e., up the roof slope from the worker) and setting up a maximum work range from the anchor point according to the manufacturer's instructions.

A **personal fall arrest system** is designed to safely stop a fall before the worker strikes a lower level. It has three major components:

A. An **anchorage** to which the lanyard's snap hook is attached.

B. A full-body **harness** worn by the worker.

C. A connector, such as a **lanyard** or **lifeline,** linking the harness to the anchorage.

Personal fall arrest systems typically use a shock-absorbing lanyard, a self-retracting lifeline, or a deceleration device.

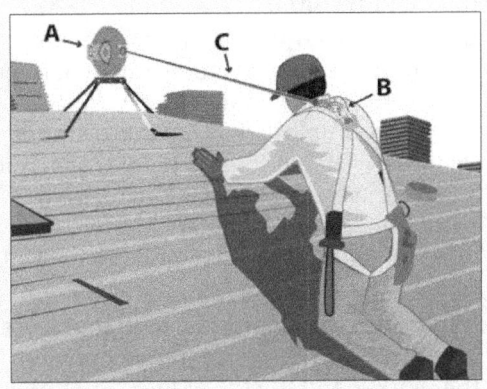

The *total fall distance* is the minimum vertical distance between the worker and a lower level that is necessary to ensure that the worker avoids contact with the lower level during a fall. It is important that employers calculate this distance before work begins to ensure that the proper fall protection equipment is selected for the location. To determine the total fall distance, several factors must be taken into consideration:

▪ **Free fall distance**: The distance the worker falls before the PFAS begins to slow the fall. This distance must be 6 feet or less for a PFAS (29 CFR 1926.502(d)(16)(iii)).

- **Deceleration distance**: The distance the lanyard stretches in order to arrest the fall. OSHA requires that this distance be no greater than 3.5 feet (29 CFR 1926.502(d)(16)(iv)), but it may be less for some PFAS equipment.
- **D-ring shift**: How far the D-ring shifts and the harness stretches when it supports the full weight of a fallen worker, including the weight of tool belts and other attached equipment or tools. Employers typically assume this shift is 1 foot, but it can vary, depending on the equipment design and the manufacturer.
- **Back D-ring height**: The height of the D-ring, measured as the distance between the D-ring and the sole of the worker's footwear. Employers often use a standard distance of 5 feet for this height, assuming a worker who is 6 feet tall. The D-ring height needs to be adjusted for very tall workers, and for shorter workers as well.
- **Safety margin**: An additional distance (typically a minimum of 2 feet) to ensure that there is enough clearance between the worker and the lower level after a fall.

The total fall clearance distance can be calculated by adding all of these values together.

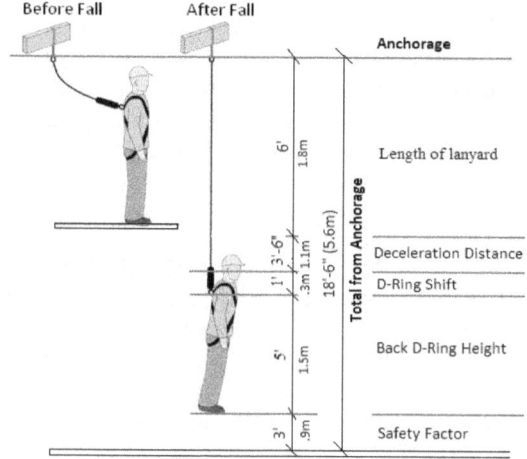

Rescue of Workers

Employers need a plan for rescuing workers in the event of a fall whenever personal fall arrest systems are used. A personal fall arrest system can save a life; however, a medical emergency, such as suspension trauma, can develop if the fallen worker is not rescued quickly. A fallen worker may not be able to reach a safe work surface without assistance. The availability of rescue personnel, ladders or other rescue equipment should be evaluated prior to starting the job. Employers need to ensure supervisors and workers are trained on how to get the fallen worker to safety. Rescues must be done promptly (29 CFR 1926.502(d)(20)) and safely to prevent further injury.

Using a Fall Restraint System

Employers can use a fall restraint system to protect workers from fall hazards. A fall restraint system stops workers from reaching the edge of the walking/working area even if they lose their footing and slide. OSHA recommends that fall restraint systems have the capacity to withstand 3,000 pounds or twice the maximum expected force needed to restrain the employee from exposure to the fall hazard. www.osha.gov/pls/oshaweb/owadisp.show_document?p_table=INTERPRETATIONS&p_id=22006.

When employers use fall restraint systems to prevent workers from reaching unprotected sides or edges, they must train workers how to determine the appropriate lanyard length prior to beginning work.

Using a Guardrail System

Employers can use guardrail systems around roof openings and at the roof perimeter to protect workers from fall hazards. Temporary guardrail systems that attach to rafters or other structural members are increasingly available through commercial sources.

The top rails of a guardrail system must be 39 to 45 inches above the walking/working surface (29 CFR 1926.502(b)(1)). Intermediate structural members (for example, midrails or screens) must be installed when there is no wall or parapet wall at least 21 inches high (29 CFR 1926.502(b)(2)). Midrails, when used, must be installed midway between the top edge of the guardrail system and the walking/ working surface (29 CFR 1926.502(b)(2)(i)).

Guardrail systems must be able to withstand a 200-pound force in any outward or downward direction within 2 inches of the top edge (29 CFR 1926.502(b)(3)).

Midrails, screens, mesh, intermediate vertical members, solid panels, and equivalent structural members must withstand a 150-pound force in any outward or downward direction (29 CFR 1926.502(b)(5)).

Guardrail systems must be surfaced to prevent punctures and lacerations and to prevent clothes from snagging (29 CFR 1926.502(b)(6)).

Warning Lines and Safety Monitors

Employers can elect to protect their workers from falling, while engaged in roofing activities on **low-slope roofs**, by a combination of warning line system and guardrail system, warning line system and safety net system, warning line system and personal fall arrest system, or warning line system and safety monitoring system. Or, on roofs 50 feet (15.25 m) or less in width, the use of a safety monitoring system alone is permitted (29 CFR 1926.501(b)(10)). The safety monitor is always a competent person (29 CFR 1926.500(b)).

The warning line system shall consist of ropes, wires, or chains, and supporting stanchions (29 CFR 1926.502(f)(2)). The warning line system shall:

- be erected not less than 6 feet (1.8 m) from the roof edge (29 CFR 1926.502(f)(1)(i)); not less than 10 feet when mechanical equipment is used (29 CFR 1926.502(f)(1)(ii));
- be flagged at least every 6 feet with high-visibility material (29 CFR 1926.502(f)(2)(i));
- be no less than 34 inches (.9 m) and no more than 39 inches (1.0 m) from the walking/working surface (29 CFR 1926.502(f)(2)(ii));
- be capable of resisting a force of at least 16 pounds (71 N) without tipping over (29 CFR 1926.502(f)(2)(iii));
- have a minimum tensile strength of 500 pounds (2.22 kN) (29 CFR 1926.502(f)(2)(iv));
- be attached in such a way that pulling on the line will not result in slack being taken up in adjacent sections before the stanchion tips over (29 CFR 1926.502(f)(2)(v)).

Covers

Employers can use covers to protect workers from falling through skylights and other holes/openings on roofs (29 CFR 1926.501(b)(4)(i)). If used the covers shall:

- be capable of supporting, without failure, at least twice the weight of employees, equipment, and materials that may be imposed on the cover at any one time (29 CFR 1926.502(i)(2));

- be secured when installed so as to prevent accidental displacement by the wind, equipment, or employees (29 CFR 1926.502(i)(3));
- be color coded or marked with the word "HOLE" or "COVER" to provide warning of the hazard (29 CFR 1926.502(i)(4)).

All Ladders

Ladders can give roofers a convenient way to access upper work levels. Extension ladders and stepladders are the two most common types of ladders on roofing job sites.

Employers must ensure that ladders are inspected by a competent person for visible defects on a periodic basis and after any occurrence that could affect their safe use (29 CFR 1926.1053(b)(15)).

The employer shall train each worker how to recognize hazards related to ladders and in the procedures to be followed to minimize those hazards (29 CFR 1926.1060(a)).

Secure footing for all ladders is important; ladders must be used only on stable and level surfaces unless they are secured to prevent accidental displacement (29 CFR 1926.1053(b)(6)). It may be necessary to take steps to create a secure footing that will support the ladder without the ladder sinking, shifting, or sliding.

Employers must ensure that areas at the top and bottom of the ladder are kept clear (29 CFR 1926.1053(b)(9)), and ladders must not be placed in areas of traffic, such as driveways or doorways, unless they are secured to prevent accidental displacement or protected from the traffic via a barricade (29 CFR 1926.1053(b)(8)).

Worker Position on a Ladder

As a good practice, employers should train workers to maintain three points of contact (two hands and a foot, or two feet and a hand) at all times when ascending or descending a ladder. Additionally, workers must not carry anything that could cause them to lose their balance and fall (29 CFR 1926.1053(b)(22)). (Workers can put tools in a bucket and use a rope to pull them up to the working level.)

Extension Ladders

Employers must ensure that non-self-supporting ladders are set at an angle so the horizontal distance between the top support and the foot of the ladder is approximately one-quarter the working length of the ladder (a 1:4 ratio) (29 CFR 1926.1053(b)(5)(i)). (The working length of the ladder is the distance along the ladder between the foot and the top support.) The side rails of the ladder generally must extend at least 3 feet above the upper landing surface that the worker is trying to access (29 CFR 1926.1053(b)(1)). When such an extension is not possible because of the ladder's length, the ladder must be secured at its top to a rigid support that will not deflect and a grasping device, such as a grabrail, must be provided to assist workers in mounting and dismounting the ladder.

Stepladders

Employers need to ensure that workers use stepladders in the fully open position. Workers must not use the top or the top step of a stepladder as a step; doing so could lead to serious injury (29 CFR 1926.1053(b)(13)).

See these additional resources related to safe ladder work practices:

- Falling Off Ladders Can Kill – Use Them Safely: www.osha.gov/Publications/OSHA3625.pdf
- Safe Use of Extension Ladders – Fact Sheet: www.osha.gov/Publications/OSHA3660.pdf
- Safe Use of Job-made Wooden Ladders – Fact Sheet: www.osha.gov/Publications/OSHA3661.pdf
- Safe Use of Stepladders – Fact Sheet: www.osha.gov/Publications/OSHA3662.pdf
- NIOSH Ladder safety app for mobile devices: www.cdc.gov/niosh/topics/falls

Additional OSHA requirements regarding ladders are provided in 29 CFR 1926.1053.

Scaffolding

Scaffolds must be designed by a qualified person and must be constructed and loaded in accord with that design (29 CFR 1926.451(a)(6)).

Employers must ensure that only experienced and trained workers erect, move, dismantle or alter scaffolds. That work must be done under the supervision and direction of a competent person qualified in scaffold erection, moving, dismantling, or alteration (29 CFR 1926.451(f)(7)).

Access

Workers are most vulnerable to fall hazards when climbing on or off a scaffold. Therefore, employers need to provide safe scaffold access. When scaffold platforms are more than 2 feet above or below a point of access, workers must use portable ladders, hook-on ladders, attachable ladders, stair towers, stairway-type ladders, ramps, walkways, integral pre-fabricated scaffold access, or direct access from another scaffold, structure, personnel hoist or similar surface (29 CFR 1926.451(e)(1)).

Platform

Employers must ensure that each platform on all working levels of scaffolds are fully planked or decked between the front uprights and the guardrail supports as per 29 CFR 1926.451(b)(1). The space between adjacent platform units and the space between the platform and the uprights must be no more than 1 inch (2.5 cm) wide, except where the employer can demonstrate that a wider space is necessary (29 CFR 1926.451(b)(1)(i)).

Guardrails

Employers must ensure that workers on a scaffold more than 10 feet above a lower level are protected from falls (29 CFR 1926.451(g)(1)). Employers often use guardrails to provide this protection.

Guardrails used to comply with OSHA's fall protection requirements for scaffolds must be installed along all open sides and ends of platforms (29 CFR 1926.451(g)(4)(i)). And generally, toprails must be installed between 36 or 38 and 45 inches above the platform surface depending on the type and age of the scaffold (29 CFR 1926.451(g)(4)(ii)). Toprails must be able to withstand, without failure, a force (applied in any downward or horizontal direction at any point along its top edge) of at least 100 pounds for single-point and two-point adjustable suspension scaffolds and of at least 200 pounds for all other scaffolds (29 CFR 1926.451(g)(4)(vii)).

When midrails are used, employers must ensure that they are installed at a height approximately midway between the top edge of the guardrail system and the platform surface (29 CFR 1926.451(g)(4)(iv)).

When screens and mesh are used, employers must ensure they extend from the top edge of the guardrail system to the scaffold platform, and along the entire opening between the supports (29 CFR 1926.451(g)(4)(v)).

Midrails, screens, mesh, intermediate vertical members, solid panels, and equivalent structural members of a guardrail system must be able to withstand, without failure, a force applied in any downward or horizontal direction at any point along the midrail or other member of at least 75 pounds for guardrail systems with a minimum 100 pound toprail capacity, and at least 150 pounds for guardrail systems with a minimum 200 pound toprail capacity (29 CFR 1926.451(g)(4)(ix)).

Falling Object Protection

Employers are required to protect workers from objects falling from scaffolds (29 CFR 1926.451(h)(1)). Where there is a danger of tools, materials, or equipment falling from a scaffold and striking workers below, employers must follow a series of requirements (29 CFR 1926.451(h)(2)). The area below the scaffold must be barricaded and workers must not enter the hazard area (29 CFR 1926.451(h)(2)(i)). Also, toeboards generally must be erected along the edge of platforms more than 10 feet above lower levels for a distance sufficient to protect workers below (29 CFR 1926.451(h)(2)(ii)). When used, toeboards must be at least 3½ inches high from the top edge of the toeboard to the level of the walking/working surface and must be securely fastened at the outermost edge of the platform and have no more than 1/4 inch clearance above the walking/working surface (29 CFR 1926.451(h)(4)(ii)).

Training

Employers must designate a qualified person to train workers how to recognize and control the hazards associated with the type of scaffold being used (29 CFR 1926.454(a)).

Employers must also designate a competent person to train workers who erect, disassemble, move, repair, maintain, operate, or inspect scaffolds to recognize any hazards associated with these activities on the scaffold systems they will use (29 CFR 1926.454(b)). Training must be provided in a language the workers being trained can understand.

Employers must retrain workers when:

- changes at the worksite present new hazards;
- changes in the type of scaffold, fall protection systems, falling object protection systems, or other equipment present new hazards; and
- inadequacies in work involving scaffolds indicate that the worker has not retained the requisite proficiency.

For additional information on what must be included in scaffold training, see 29 CFR 1926.454 – Training Requirements.

Lifts

Aerial Lifts

Employers can use aerial lifts to enable workers to work at the edge of a roof while standing in the lift basket. Employers must only permit authorized workers to operate extensible and articulating boom platforms (29 CFR 1926.453(b)(2)(ii)). Employers must ensure that the controls for extending and articulating arms are tested daily before use to be sure that they are functioning safely (29 CFR 1926.453(b)(2)(i)).

With respect to extensible and articulating boom platforms, employers must ensure that:

- workers stand firmly on the basket floor and do not sit or climb on the edge of the basket or use planks, ladders, or other devices for a work position (29 CFR 1926.453(b)(2)(iv)); and
- workers are tied-off to the boom or basket (29 CFR 1926.453(b)(2)(v)).

See additional OSHA requirements for aerial lifts in 29 CFR 1926.453.

All-Terrain Forklifts

All-terrain forklifts are covered under 29 CFR 1926.602(c). Employers use these vehicles for raising equipment and materials to the roof and, in conjunction with manufacturer-approved man-baskets, to raise workers (29 CFR 1926.602(c)(1)(ii)). When elevating workers, a safety platform firmly secured to the lifting carriage and/or forks must be used (29 CFR 1926.602(c)(1)(viii)(A)).

Employers must ensure that forklift operators are appropriately trained (29 CFR 1926.602(d); 29 CFR 1910.178(l)).

Safe Debris Disposal

Employers must consider worker safety when selecting a method for handling debris. If not managed properly, debris can become a trip hazard and contribute to falls. Falling debris can hit workers on the ground below. One effective method employers can use to manage debris is to use a forklift to raise a collection box to the roof level. When the box is full, or when the job is complete, the box of debris can be lowered to the ground without putting workers at risk. As an added benefit, this practice makes the cleanup process more efficient.

Electrical Safety

Most electrocutions involving roofers usually result from contact with overhead powerlines (service drops are the most common). Workers can also be exposed to potential electrocution hazards by contacting electrical conduit that may be buried in old roofing material that must be removed. Employers must protect workers from electrical hazards by de-energizing the circuits, grounding, or by guarding it effectively by insulation (29 CFR 1926.416(a)(1)).

See additional requirements related to electrical safety under 29 CFR 1926, Subpart K.

Integrity of Older Buildings

Before work begins, employers must ensure that any roof to be worked on has the strength and structural integrity to safely support workers (29 CFR 1926.501(a)(2)). Sometimes it may be necessary to inspect a roof from the inside of the structure to identify integrity issues.

Roofing Operations

Built-up Roofing

While hot tar built-up roofing represents a small percentage of residential work, it is used often in commercial roofing.

Working with hot tar at 500°F can cause severe burns if the tar is mishandled.

Fires are obvious hazards around kettles and tankers. Fire prevention is critical during hot work. A kettle can catch fire or even explode if the tar heats to its flash point. Employers must develop a fire protection program that includes provisions for required firefighting equipment at their job sites (29 CFR 1926.150(a)(1)).

Employers must have fire extinguishers, rated not less than 10B, within 50 feet of wherever more than 5 gallons of flammable or combustible liquids or 5 pounds of flammable gas are being used on the job site (29 CFR 1926.150(c)(1)(vi)). Employers should also ensure that workers follow the precautions specified by the manufacturer of the bitumen and the kettle.

Employers must ensure that workers are trained to operate equipment safely and to identify and avoid hazards (29 CFR 1926.20(b)(4) and 29 CFR 1926.21(b)(2)).

Because of the nature of built-up roofing work, employers need to provide necessary personal protective equipment. Working around kettles, tankers, luggers, and mop buckets can lead to spills and splashes from hot tar. To protect workers from burns, proper clothing like gloves, work boots, long sleeve cotton shirts, long cotton pants without cuffs, eye protection or face shields must be provided.

Torch Applied Roofing

Torch applied roofing uses an open flame system that can reach temperatures of 2,000°F at the torch end. When heat from the torch is improperly applied to the roofing ply, it can conduct enough heat to ignite combustible materials underneath, such as wood decking or trusses, without the knowledge of the roofer. Preconstruction surveys, following the ply manufacturer's application techniques, and posting a fire watch can prevent a catastrophic loss and personal injury from fires. Regular fire-watch inspections should be done throughout the day by a competent person and for a minimum of two hours starting when the last torch is extinguished on a roof. Inspections should include the roof's entire field, flashings and the underside of the roof deck.

Working around unprotected or improperly stored propane tanks is a recipe for a serious accident. Never heat a propane tank with a torch, lay a tank on its side, or use the wrong gauge or pressure beyond the specifications of the tank or application instructions.

Employers must ensure that propane tank storage meets local building codes and OSHA requirements at 29 CFR 1926.153(j), 29 CFR 1926.153(k) and 29 CFR 1926.153(l).

Single-ply Roofing

While there are some single-ply roofing applications that involve hot work, most applications of single-ply roofing use solvent-based adhesives. These adhesives are usually highly flammable. Employers need to ensure that open flames and smoking are not permitted while these adhesives are used.

Employers need to ensure that workers understand the warnings on the adhesive container labels and follow the personal protective equipment (PPE) handling and use recommendations found in the applicable safety data sheets (SDSs).

Roofing Tool Safety

Roofing hand and power tools and equipment can be hazardous and can cause severe injuries if used incorrectly. Employers can reduce the risk of injuries by providing tool guards, PPE and training workers.

Power tools (e.g., nail guns, saws, etc.) should have the proper shields, guards, or safety attachments specified by the manufacturer. Employers must ensure that workers using power tools wear appropriate eye protection (29 CFR 1926.102(a)(1)). Always be sure to replace damaged or missing tool guards (29 CFR 1926.300(b)(1)).

Employers need to train workers on the proper use of roofing tools and equipment. In this training, it is important to discuss tool safety features, safe operating procedures, and safe work practices, such as proper body placement and how to use PPE.

Personal Protective Equipment

Employers have a duty to protect workers from recognized hazards. Where the hazard cannot be eliminated by other types of controls (e.g., engineering or administrative controls), employers must ensure that workers wear appropriate PPE (29 CFR 1926.28 and 29 CFR 1926.95). Employers need to ensure that workers are properly trained in the inspection, care, fit and use of required PPE.

- **Nail guns:** Wear hearing protection and eye protection. Also use safety devices that prevent the nail gun from discharging unless it is in contact with the work surface. Avoid carrying the nail gun against the body, or with a finger on the trigger, or while connected to the air compressor.

See Publication on Nail Guns on OSHA's website at: www.osha.gov/doc/topics/nailgun

- **Generator/air compressor:** Wear hearing protection and eye protection while working near the equipment.
- **Compressed air:** Wear hearing protection and eye protection. Also use a whip check or wire connections to prevent separation. Confirm that the pressure is adjusted appropriately for the tool.
- **Shingle stripper (manual):** Wear proper footwear and eye protection.
- **Tin snips:** Wear work gloves and safety glasses. Discard waste or scrap metal appropriately.
- **Power saw:** Wear hearing protection, eye protection, and work gloves. Ensure that blades are sharp and that guards are in place and functioning correctly.
- **Working near mobile equipment or traffic:** Wear high-visibility clothing (e.g., vest).
- **Unprotected work at heights 6 feet or greater:** Use fall arrest or fall restraint equipment.
- **Hazardous substance present:** Wear an appropriate respirator[1] if permissible dust, mist, or fume levels are exceeded.
- **General:** Employers must determine when it is appropriate for workers to wear hard hats, safety glasses, and work boots. Additionally, workers should know how to inspect the PPE and put it on so that it will protect them from the hazards they could encounter at the work site.

---

[1] Workers who are required to wear respirators must be covered by a respiratory protection program and meet other requirements of 29 CFR 1926.103 and 29 CFR 1910.134 – Respiratory Protection.

Protecting Workers Who Work with Hazardous Substances

Hazard Communication

If workers are exposed to hazardous substances, their employers must develop a hazard communication program that trains workers how to read and understand safety data sheets, container labeling, and other forms of warning. The training must also include the measures workers must use to protect themselves. The employer also must share information about hazardous chemicals with other employers whose workers on the site could be exposed. See 29 CFR 1926.59 and 29 CFR 1910.1200.

Specific Health Hazards

Roofers may come across hazardous chemicals such as:

- **Asbestos** – Asbestos enters the body primarily through inhalation. It can also enter the digestive tract if workers eat or smoke in a contaminated area. Breathing asbestos fibers can cause a buildup of scar-like tissue in the lungs called "asbestosis" and result in loss of lung function that often progresses to disability and death. Asbestos also causes cancer of the lung and other diseases. Employers must protect roofers from asbestos exposure which is found in some insulation products and other roofing and siding materials on older homes. For protection requirements related to working with asbestos-containing materials, see 29 CFR 1926.1101 – Asbestos.

- **Lead** – Lead enters the body primarily through inhalation and ingestion. Workers are mainly exposed to lead by breathing in lead-containing dust and fumes. Lead passes through the lungs into the blood where it can harm many of the body's organ systems. Employers must protect roofers from lead exposure which is found in lead-based paints, including old paint on exposed woodwork and steel. For protection requirements related to working with lead-containing materials, see 29 CFR 1926.62 – Lead.

- **Silica** – Workers who inhale very small crystalline silica particles are at risk for silicosis. Symptoms of silicosis can include shortness of breath, cough and fatigue, and may or may not be obviously attributable to silica. Workers exposed to airborne crystalline silica also are at increased risk for lung cancer, chronic obstructive pulmonary disease and kidney disease. Employers must protect roofers from silica exposure which may be found in concrete and ceramic roof tiles. For protection requirements related to working with silica-containing materials, see 29 CFR 1926.55 – Appendix A, Gases, Vapors, Fumes, Dusts and Mists.

- **Other.** See 29 CFR 1926.55 – Appendix A, Gases, Vapors, Fumes, Dusts and Mists.

Coordinating with Other Contractors

All contractors on site need to be aware of all operations. For example, contractors should be aware of other employers' barricaded areas so as to minimize the possibility of workers being hit by falling debris or being struck by moving equipment.

Housekeeping

Effective housekeeping will help keep the worksite organized and minimize hazards that may cause workers to trip or fall. Specifically, watch for loose cords and air hoses that can roll underfoot and cause workers to lose their footing on a roof. Keep supplies and hand tools secured so that they do not present a tripping hazard. Secure tools when not in use to ensure that they will not fall off the roof. See 29 CFR 1926.25.

Emergency Action Plan (EAP)

Emergency Services

Employers must train workers in any emergency action plan required by OSHA standards (29 CFR 1926.35(e)(2)). EAPs must include, among other information, the preferred means of reporting emergencies and procedures for evacuating the area (29 CFR 1926.35(b)). Workers should always know the street address of where they are working in case they need to give emergency services their location. Post the site street address and emergency contact information in prominent locations. This will allow workers to quickly contact emergency services with necessary information.

First Aid and Medical Emergencies

When there is no infirmary, clinic, hospital, or physician within a reasonably accessible time and distance, employers must ensure that someone is available at the site with first-aid training verified by documentary evidence (such as a training certificate) (29 CFR 1926.50(c)). Required first-aid supplies must be easily accessible (29 CFR 1926.50(d)(1)). Where the eyes or body of any person may be exposed to injurious corrosive materials, suitable facilities for quick drenching or flushing of the eyes and body must be provided within the work area for immediate emergency use (29 CFR 1926.50(g)). See 29 CFR 1926.50 – Medical Services and First Aid, for additional requirements.

General Duty to Protect Workers from Other Hazards

Roofers are routinely exposed to the elements, which means there is often a threat of overexposure to hot or cold conditions, the sun, or stinging or biting insects. Employers have a duty to protect workers from recognized serious hazards on the job site (Section 5(a)(1) of the *Occupational Safety and Health Act*).

Heat Illnesses

Every year, thousands of workers become sick from occupational heat exposure, and some even die. These illnesses and deaths are preventable. Symptoms of heat illnesses include:

- Throbbing headache
- Dizziness and light-headedness
- Lack of sweating despite the heat
- Red, hot, and dry skin
- Muscle weakness or cramps
- Nausea and vomiting
- Rapid heartbeat, which may be either strong or weak
- Rapid, shallow breathing
- Behavioral changes such as confusion, disorientation, or staggering
- Seizures
- Unconsciousness

Employers should plan for preventing — and treating workers who are experiencing symptoms of — heat-related illnesses. Heat illnesses range from heat rash and heat cramps to heat exhaustion and heat stroke. Heat stroke requires immediate medical attention and can result in death. Employers should provide workers with water, rest and shade; should gradually increase workloads and allow more frequent breaks for new workers or workers who have been away for a week or more (acclimatization); and should educate workers about the symptoms of heat-related illnesses and how to prevent them. Always remember: WATER, REST, SHADE.

Note: Get more information on how to prevent heat illnesses, as well as planning and training resources, from OSHA's Heat Illness Prevention website at www.osha.gov/heat.

Cold Stress

Prolonged exposure to freezing or cold temperatures can cause serious health problems such as trench foot, frostbite and hypothermia. In extreme cases, including cold water immersion, exposure can lead to death. Employers need to train workers how to recognize the danger signs of cold stress, which can include uncontrolled shivering, slurred speech, clumsy movements, fatigue, and confused behavior. If these signs are observed, workers should know how to get emergency help.

Note: Get more information on how to prevent cold weather injuries, illnesses and fatalities, as well as planning and training resources, from OSHA's Winter Weather website: www.osha.gov/dts/weather/winter_weather.

Other Weather Conditions

High winds, wet weather, and icy conditions are especially hazardous for roofing workers. It is important for employers to consider suspending operations in bad weather. This is especially important when working on any roofing surface that can be particularly slippery when wet, including slate, tile, metal roofs and some single ply membranes.

Workers' Rights

Workers have the right to:

- Working conditions that do not pose a risk of serious harm.
- Receive information and training (in a language and vocabulary the worker understands) about workplace hazards, methods to prevent them, and the OSHA standards that apply to their workplace.
- Review records of work-related injuries and illnesses.
- File a complaint asking OSHA to inspect their workplace if they believe there is a serious hazard or that their employer is not following OSHA's rules. OSHA will keep all identities confidential.
- Exercise their rights under the law without retaliation, including reporting an injury or raising health and safety concerns with their employer or OSHA. If a worker has been retaliated against for using their rights, they must file a complaint with OSHA as soon as possible, but no later than 30 days.

For more information, see OSHA's Workers page.

OSHA Assistance, Services and Programs

OSHA has a great deal of information to assist employers in complying with their responsibilities under OSHA law. Several OSHA programs and services can help employers identify and correct job hazards, as well as improve their injury and illness prevention program.

Establishing an Injury and Illness Prevention Program

The key to a safe and healthful work environment is a comprehensive injury and illness prevention program.

Injury and illness prevention programs are systems that can substantially reduce the number and severity of workplace injuries and illnesses, while reducing costs to employers. Thousands of employers across the United States already manage safety using injury and illness prevention programs, and OSHA believes that all employers can and should do the same. Thirty-four states have requirements or voluntary guidelines for workplace injury and illness prevention programs. Most successful injury and illness prevention programs are based on a common set of key elements. These include management leadership, worker participation, hazard identification, hazard prevention and control, education and training, and program evaluation and improvement. Visit OSHA's Injury and Illness Prevention Programs web page at www.osha.gov/dsg/topics/safetyhealth for more information.

Compliance Assistance Specialists

OSHA has compliance assistance specialists throughout the nation located in most OSHA offices. Compliance assistance specialists can provide information to employers and workers about OSHA standards, short educational programs on specific hazards or OSHA rights and responsibilities, and information on additional compliance assistance resources. For more details, visit www.osha.gov/dcsp/compliance_assistance/cas.html or call 1-800-321-OSHA (6742) to contact your local OSHA office.

Free On-site Safety and Health Consultation Services for Small Business

OSHA's On-site Consultation Program offers free and confidential advice to small and medium-sized businesses in all states across the country, with priority given to high-hazard worksites. Each year, responding to requests from small employers looking to create or improve their safety and health management programs, OSHA's On-site Consultation Program conducts over 29,000 visits to small business worksites covering over 1.5 million workers across the nation.

On-site consultation services are separate from enforcement and do not result in penalties or citations. Consultants from state agencies or universities work with employers to identify workplace hazards, provide advice on compliance with OSHA standards, and assist in establishing safety and health management programs.

For more information, to find the local On-site Consultation office in your state, or to request a brochure on Consultation Services, visit www.osha.gov/consultation, or call 1-800-321-OSHA (6742).

Under the consultation program, certain exemplary employers may request participation in OSHA's **Safety and Health Achievement Recognition Program (SHARP)**. Eligibility for participation includes, but is not limited to, receiving a full-service, comprehensive consultation visit, correcting all identified hazards and developing an effective safety and health management program. Worksites that receive SHARP recognition are exempt from programmed inspections during the period that the SHARP certification is valid.

Occupational Safety and Health Training Courses

The OSHA Training Institute partners with 27 OSHA Training Institute Education Centers at 42 locations throughout the United States to deliver courses on OSHA standards and occupational safety and health topics to thousands of students a year. For more information on training courses, visit www.osha.gov/otiec.

OSHA Educational Materials

OSHA has many types of educational materials in English, Spanish, Vietnamese and other languages available in print or online. These include:

- Brochures/booklets;
- Fact Sheets;
- Guidance documents that provide detailed examinations of specific safety and health issues;
- Online Safety and Health Topics pages;
- Posters;
- Small, laminated QuickCards™ that provide brief safety and health information; and
- *QuickTakes*, OSHA's free, twice-monthly online newsletter with the latest news about OSHA initiatives and products to assist employers and workers in finding and preventing workplace hazards. To sign up for *QuickTakes* visit www.osha.gov/quicktakes.

To view materials available online or for a listing of free publications, visit www.osha.gov/publications. You can also call 1-800-321-OSHA (6742) to order publications.

OSHA's web site also has information on job hazards and injury and illness prevention for employers and workers. To learn more about OSHA's safety and health resources online, visit www.osha.gov. Use the A-Z index to help find information and assistance.

NIOSH Health Hazard Evaluation Program

Getting Help with Health Hazards

The National Institute for Occupational Safety and Health (NIOSH) is a federal agency that conducts scientific and medical research on workers' safety and health. At no cost to employers or workers, NIOSH can help identify health hazards and recommend ways to reduce or eliminate those hazards in the workplace through its Health Hazard Evaluation (HHE) Program.

Workers, union representatives and employers can request a NIOSH HHE. An HHE is often requested when there is a higher than expected rate of a disease or injury in a group of workers. These situations may be the result of an unknown cause, a new hazard, or a mixture of sources. To request a NIOSH Health Hazard Evaluation go to www.cdc. gov/niosh/hhe/request.html. To find out more about the Health Hazard Evaluation Program:

- Call (513) 841-4382, or to talk to a staff member in Spanish, call (513) 841-4439; or
- Send an email to HHERequestHelp@cdc.gov.

OSHA Regional Offices

Region I
Boston Regional Office
(CT*, ME, MA, NH, RI, VT*)
JFK Federal Building, Room E340
Boston, MA 02203
(617) 565-9860 (617) 565-9827 Fax

Region II
New York Regional Office
(NJ*, NY*, PR*, VI*)
201 Varick Street, Room 670
New York, NY 10014
(212) 337-2378 (212) 337-2371 Fax

Region III
Philadelphia Regional Office
(DE, DC, MD*, PA, VA*, WV)
The Curtis Center
170 S. Independence Mall West
Suite 740 West
Philadelphia, PA 19106-3309
(215) 861-4900 (215) 861-4904 Fax

Region IV
Atlanta Regional Office
(AL, FL, GA, KY*, MS, NC*, SC*, TN*)
61 Forsyth Street, SW, Room 6T50
Atlanta, GA 30303
(678) 237-0400 (678) 237-0447 Fax

Region V
Chicago Regional Office
(IL*, IN*, MI*, MN*, OH, WI)
230 South Dearborn Street
Room 3244
Chicago, IL 60604
(312) 353-2220 (312) 353-7774 Fax

Region VI
Dallas Regional Office
(AR, LA, NM*, OK, TX)
525 Griffin Street, Room 602
Dallas, TX 75202
(972) 850-4145 (972) 850-4149 Fax
(972) 850-4150 FSO Fax

Region VII
Kansas City Regional Office
(IA*, KS, MO, NE)
Two Pershing Square Building
2300 Main Street, Suite 1010
Kansas City, MO 64108-2416
(816) 283-8745 (816) 283-0547 Fax

Region VIII
Denver Regional Office
(CO, MT, ND, SD, UT*, WY*)
Cesar Chavez Memorial Building
1244 Speer Boulevard, Suite 551
Denver, CO 80204
(720) 264-6550 (720) 264-6585 Fax

Region IX
San Francisco Regional Office
(AZ*, CA*, HI*, NV*, and American Samoa,
Guam and the Northern Mariana Islands)
90 7th Street, Suite 18100
San Francisco, CA 94103
(415) 625-2547 (415) 625-2534 Fax

Region X
Seattle Regional Office
(AK*, ID, OR*, WA*)
300 Fifth Avenue, Suite 1280
Seattle, WA 98104
(206) 757-6700 (206) 757-6705 Fax

* These states and territories operate their own OSHA-approved job safety and health plans and cover state and local government employees as well as private sector employees. The Connecticut, Illinois, New Jersey, New York and Virgin Islands programs cover public employees only. (Private sector workers in these states are covered by Federal OSHA). States with approved programs must have standards that are identical to, or at least as effective as, the Federal OSHA standards.

Note: To get contact information for OSHA area offices, OSHA-approved state plans and OSHA consultation projects, please visit us online at www.osha.gov or call us at 1-800-321-OSHA (6742).

How to Contact OSHA

For questions or to get information or advice, to report an emergency, report a fatality or catastrophe, order publications, sign up for OSHA's e-newsletter *QuickTakes*, or to file a confidential complaint, contact your nearest OSHA office, visit www.osha.gov or call OSHA at 1-800-321-OSHA (6742), TTY 1-877-889-5627.

**For assistance, contact us.
We are OSHA. We can help.**

www.ingramcontent.com/pod-product-compliance
Lightning Source LLC
Chambersburg PA
CBHW070923180526
45168CB00005B/2132